OLD MASTER DRAWINGS

OLD MASTER DRAWINGS

FROM THE COLLECTION OF MR. & MRS. LESTER FRANCIS AVNET

CIRCULATED BY THE AMERICAN FEDERATION OF ARTS, NEW YORK

©1968 The American Federation of Arts
41 East 65th Street, New York, New York 10021
Library of Congress Catalog Card Number 72-76721
Type Set by Volk & Huxley Typographers, New York
Printed by Sanders Printing Corporation, New York
Edited by Marian G. Ruggles
Designed by Lorraine Jurian
Photographs by Charles Uht, New York, with the exception of the
following: (4, 6, 12-13, 20, 22, 36, 40-41, 44-45, 74, 81, 103);
Courtesy of Wildenstein and Co., Inc., New York
Exhibition number 69-16/Circulated 1969-70

Mr. and Mrs. Lester Avnet's fine 19th and 20th century drawings have become known throughout the United States in the last year through an exhibition entitled *Figures and Faces* which has been circulated by the American Federation of Arts. The present exhibition, larger in size and scope, now introduces us to another facet of the Avnet's Collection — drawings by Old Masters.

The one hundred drawings by some sixty artists who reached their maturity before 1800 represent the achievement of this collector's eye during the last decade. Spanning over three centuries, from the Bellini *Profile Portrait of a Young Man* to the three portraits by Ingres, the Avnet Collection includes unusual and masterful drawings by French, Italian, German, Swiss, Flemish, Dutch, Danish, British and American artists. From the earliest acquisitions, drawings by Boucher and Fragonard, to the most recent, pastel portraits by Chardin, the Avnets have been interested in examples of unusual quality and rarity of each master's oeuvre.

Interested in having their Collection seen by the public, the Avnets have always been generous in lending works to museums and galleries throughout the United States and also in Europe. We are grateful to them for their enthusiasm for collecting, their generosity in exhibiting, as well as for their spirit and energy which have played so great a part in the organization of this exhibition.

E. R. Hunter
Director
Norton Gallery and
School of Art

Rembrandt Harmensz van Rijn
(Dutch; 1606-1669)

Frontispiece, 79
An Oriental in Turban and Coat with a Stick
(1643/44)
pen and brown ink and wash
5⅛" x 3⁷/₁₆"

Stamp of the A. P. F. Robert-Dumesnil Collection at the center
of the bottom edge (Lugt 2200).

Provenance: A. P. F. Robert Dumesnil, Paris; François
Courboin, Paris; Wildenstein and Co., New York
Literature: Alfassa, Paul. "Les Dessins de Rembrandt."
La Revue de l'Art Ancienne et Moderne. Paris, 1908, Vol. XXIII,
p. 363; Bouyer, R. "Bibliographie – 'La Sculpture Italiene et la
Peinture Hollandaise,' par Clotilde Briere-Misme...1927."
La Revue de l'Art Ancienne et Moderne. Paris, 1927, Vol.LII,
p. 191; Benesch, Otto. *Rembrandt, Werk und Forschung.* Vienna,
1935, p. 36; Benesch, Otto. *The Drawings of Rembrandt. The
Middle Period: 1640-1650.* Vol. IV, 1955, #691, Fig. 828.
Exhibited: Bibliothèque Nationale, Paris. Exposition d'Oeuvres
de Rembrandt, Dessins et Gravures. May-June, 1908, cat. #385,
ill. between pp. 36-37.

ANONYMOUS
(Northern Italian; late 16th Century)

1. *Three Men Singing*
sepia
8½″ x 6½″

Inscribed at the lower right: *Theodo ?*. Inscribed on the verso:
propert of S. Francis . . . . Stamp of the August Grahl Collection
at the lower left (Lugt 1199).

This composition of the "Three Men Singing" was engraved by
Marc Antonio Raimondi in the early 16th century (see: Bartsch,
Adam. *Le Peintre Graveur.* Leipzig, 1867, Vol. 14, pp. 348-9) after
a drawing done either earlier in his career or one by his master
Francesco Raibolini, Il Francia. An engraving, now in the
collection of the Philadelphia Museum of Art, was executed
after the Raimondi around 1530 by the Master ENSR. The Avnet
drawing is believed to have been based on this later engraving.

PROVENANCE: This drawing, once part of the collection of
August Grahl of Dresden, was acquired by the Avnets in 1967
from the Swetzoff Gallery in Boston.
LITERATURE: *Catalogue of the Collection of Drawings by the Old
Masters Formed by the late Professor August Grahl of Dresden.*
Sotheby & Co., London, April 27-28, 1885, #108 (as Francesco
Raibolini, Il Francia).

DOMENICO BECCAFUMI
(Italian; ca. 1486-1551)

2. *Arched Entrance to a Medici Palace*

black chalk, pen and brown ink with brown wash
8¼" x 5½" (sight)

Mark of the Coghlan Briscoe Collection at the lower left
(Lugt supplement 347c).

This drawing was formerly page 88 of a sketchbook that
Domenico Beccafumi used throughout his life. The Medici
coat-of-arms appears directly above the arch.

PROVENANCE: George Hibbert, London; Coghlan Briscoe,
Ireland; Dr. W. M. Crofton; Thomas Agnew and Sons, London;
R. M. Light and Co., Boston
LITERATURE: Rasthoff, Rinaldo de Liphart. "Un Libro di Schizzi
di Domenico Beccafumi." *Rivista d'Arte,* 1935, p. 198, fig. 59;
Sanminiatelli, Donato. "The Beginnings of Domenico
Beccafumi." *Burlington Magazine,* Vol. XCIV, No. 657, December,
1957, pp. 401-410; *Catalogue of Important Old Master Drawings.*
Christie, Manson and Woods, Ltd., London, July, 1959, Lot 95,
#88; *Domenico Beccafumi. 1486-1551. Drawings from a Sketchbook.*
Thos. Agnew and Sons, Ltd., London, November, 1965, #7.

JACOPO BELLINI
(Italian; ca. 1400-ca. 1470)

3. *Profile Portrait of a Young Man*
pen and brown ink
12⅛" x 8⅛"

This drawing was authenticated by Bernard Berenson in
January, 1965. Another version of it, in silverpoint, is in the
Louvre Sketchbook (see: Moschini, Vittorio. *Disegni di Jacopo
Bellini*. Bergamo, 1943, Plate 28).

PROVENANCE: Wildenstein and Co., New York
LITERATURE: *Art News*. Vol. 54, No. 8, December, 1955, p. 51.
EXHIBITED: Wildenstein and Co., New York. *Timeless Master
Drawings*. November-December, 1955, cat. #5; Wildenstein and
Co., London. *Drawings by the Masters, XVth to XIXth
Centuries*. October 5-29, 1960, cat. #2; University of Pittsburgh,
May, 1965, (no catalogue).

FRANÇOIS BOUCHER
(French; 1703-1770)

5. *Les Crêpes*
pen and brown wash
13⁵/₈″ x 9¹/₈″

PROVENANCE: M. Randon de Boisset; Chevalier Lambert;
Marquess of Landsdowne; Wildenstein and Co., New York
LITERATURE: Michel, André. *François Boucher.* Paris, n.d.,
catalogue p. 72, #1299; *Vente Randon de Boisset.* Paris, February
27, 1777, pp. 133-4, #342; *Vente Chevalier Lambert.* Paris, March
27, 1787, p. 95, #232.
EXHIBITED: Charles E. Slatkin, New York. *François Boucher: An
Exhibition of Prints and Drawings.* January 28 — February 23,
1957, Plate XVIII; Caracas. *Exposicion de Dibujos del Renacimiento
al Siglo XX.* May 24-June 9, 1957, cat. #6.

FRANÇOIS BOUCHER
(French; 1703-1770)

6. *Study of a Baby*
black and white chalks on buff paper
9¼" x 11¼" (sight)

Inscribed at the lower right in ink: *Boucher.*

A similar attribution, or signature, has also been seen on the
following works sold at Sotheby and Co., London: Two putti
(June 10, 1959, Lot 4); 2 studies for decorative panels (October
16, 1963, Lots 237 & 238); "A Peasant Family Resting by a Barn"
(March 11, 1964, Lot 209).

PROVENANCE: Miss Helen A. Clark, Toronto, Canada
LITERATURE: *Catalogue of Important Old Master Drawings.*
Sotheby & Co., London, November 11, 1965, #66, ill.

POLIDORO DA CARAVAGGIO CALDARA
(Italian; 1492-1543)

7. *Study of a Seated Woman with a Child*
black chalk with touches of pen and ink
8³⁄₁₆″ x 8³⁄₄″

Stamp of the Richard Cosway Collection at the center of the
bottom edge (Lugt 628). Stamp of an unidentified collection at
the lower right.

This work is stylistically close to studies in the British Museum,
especially "A Schoolmistress with her Pupils" (see: Pouncey,
P. and J. A. Gere. *Italian Drawings...in the British Museum,
Raphael and his Circle*....Plate 182).

PROVENANCE: Richard Cosway, London; A. F. Cresswell; E. A.
Wrangham, Esq.
LITERATURE: *Catalogue of Old Master Drawings.* Sotheby & Co.,
London, July 1, 1965, #8, ill.

Luca Cambiaso
(Italian; 1527-1585)

8. *The Flagellation*
pen and brown ink and wash
7½" x 5¼" (sight)

Stamp of the Comte (?) Gelozzi (or Gelosi) Collection at the lower right (Lugt 513). Unidentified collection stamp at the lower left.

The Albertina in Vienna has a drawing by Cambiaso of the same subject showing the figures of Christ and the soldier on the left in similar positions (see: Suida Manning, Bertina and William Suida. *Luca Cambiaso, la Vita e le Opere*. Milan, 1958, fig. 388).

LITERATURE: *Catalogue of Fine Old Master Drawings.* Sotheby & Co., London, July 7, 1966, #110.

Agostino Carracci
(Italian; 1557-1602)

9. *Saint Jerome in Penitence*
black chalk on buff paper
15⅝" x 11¹⁵/₁₆"

Provenance: Michael Jaffé, Esq., Cambridge, England
Literature: *Catalogue of Important Old Master Drawings.*
Sotheby & Co., London, November 11, 1965, #54, ill.; *Arts
Magazine.* Vol. 40, No. 1, November, 1965, p. 11.

ANNIBALE CARRACCI
(Italian; 1560-1609)

10. *Landscape with Two Musicians*
pen and brown ink
$10^{11}/_{16}$″ x $16^{3}/_{16}$″ (sight)

The attribution of this drawing to Annibale Carracci was
made by A. E. Popham.

PROVENANCE: Seiferheld and Co., New York; Bianchini Gallery,
New York

JOHN SINGLETON COPLEY
(American; 1737-1815)

13. *Benjamin Franklin*
pencil
12½" x 17³⁄₁₆" (sight)

This drawing shows Franklin with his kite, with which in
1791 in Philadelphia, he proved the existence of electricity in
storm clouds.

PROVENANCE: Mr. A. Moll, Genoa, Italy
LITERATURE: *Catalogue of Fine English and Nineteenth Century
Drawings and Paintings.* Sotheby & Co., London, November 24,
1965, #33.

MICHEL CORNEILLE, THE ELDER
(French; 1642-1708)

14. *Rocky Landscape with Winding Road*
pen and brown ink over red chalk
7$^7/_{16}$" x 10$^1/_8$"

Signed with the artist's monogram on the tree trunk at the
left: *MC*. Inscribed on the mount: *Michel Corneille dit le Vieux*.

PROVENANCE: Prouté, Paris; Mr. and Mrs. Robert Laurent,
Indiana; ACA Heritage Gallery, New York
EXHIBITED: John Herron Art Museum, Indianapolis. *European
Old Master Drawings in Indiana Collections*. March 6-April 10,
1955, cat. #41, ill.

PIETRO BERRETTINI DA CORTONA
(Italian; 1596-1669)

15. *Two Angels*
black chalk heightened with white on grey-blue paper
7³/₄″ x 7³/₈″ (sight)

This is considered to be a late drawing, possibly connected
with the decoration of the apse of the Chiesa Nuova in Rome.

PROVENANCE: This drawing is one of a group of drawings which
was part of the collection of King Philip V of Spain. The album
from which they were taken bore the Spanish royal coat-of-
arms used from 1700 until 1714, when the arms of the Duchy
of Milan, ceded by Austria, were removed. It is possible that
the collection was assembled during those years. The album
may have been in the Orleans collection before passing into
English hands at the beginning of the 19th Century. Each
drawing was mounted on a numbered sheet. The Avnet drawing
is number 54.
LITERATURE: *Drawings by Old Masters*. Christie, Manson and
Woods, Ltd., London, November 22, 1966, pp. 16 & 19, #85, ill.

Antoine Coypel
(French; 1661-1722)

16. *A Nymph, Seen from Behind, Leaving a Pool*
black, white and red chalks on light blue paper
12$\frac{5}{16}$" x 9$\frac{9}{16}$" (sight)

Stamp of the William Bates Collection at the lower right (Lugt 2604). With an old attribution under the mount: *N. le Sueur.*

PROVENANCE: William Bates, Birmingham, England
LITERATURE: *Catalogue of Fine Old Master Drawings.* Sotheby & Co., London, July 7, 1966, #97.

DONATO CRETI
(Italian; 1671-1749)

17. *A Bishop and Other Figures before a Church*
pen and brown ink and grey wash
6¾" x 9¹/₁₆"

Stamp of the H. E. Field Collection at the lower right (Lugt supplement 1287). With an attribution on the verso: *Donato Creti.*

Prior to its exhibition at the John Herron Art Museum in 1955 (see below) Otto Benesch, Max J. Friedländer and Hermann Voss stated that they were inclined to accept the attribution of this drawing to Creti.

PROVENANCE: H. E. Field, New York; Prouté, Paris; Mr. and Mrs. Robert Laurent, Indiana; ACA Heritage Gallery, New York
EXHIBITED: John Herron Art Museum, Indianapolis. *European Old Master Drawings in Indiana Collections.* March 6-April 10, 1955, cat. #43, ill.

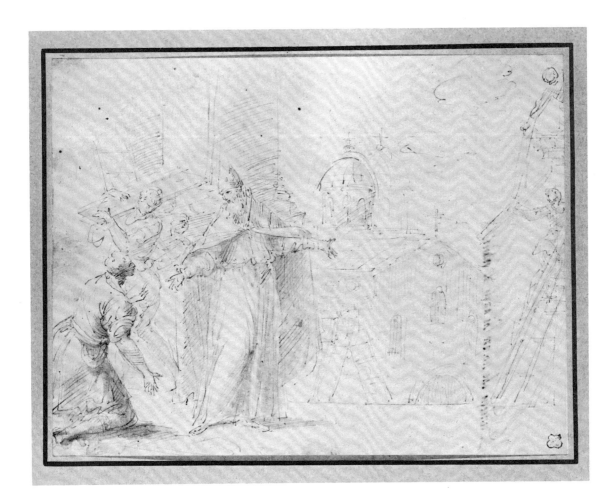

JOHN DOWNMAN
(British; 1750-1824)

18. *Portrait of Sir William Twysden of Royden Hall, Kent, and his Wife, Frances*
1786, dated
black chalk and watercolour heightened with white
20½" x 14¼" (sight)

Signed and dated in ink at the center of the left edge: *J. Downman Pt 1786*. Ink inscription on a sticker on the verso: *Sir William and Lady Twysden of Royden Hall, Kent. Painted by Downman on their marriage, May, 1786. Sir William J ? Twysden, Bart, Born 13th May 1760. Married May 1786. Frances, Daughter of Alexander Wynch Esq. Governor of Madras. (M. S. 1891.)*

PROVENANCE: Mary Montgomerie, Lady Currie; E. M. Hodgkins; John Wentworth Smith, Esq.
LITERATURE: *Important English Drawings and Watercolours.* Christie, Manson and Woods Ltd., London, March 19, 1968, #140, ill.

Jean-Honoré Fragonard
(French; 1732-1806)

19. *Education of the Virgin*
(1764)
charcoal
10$^{15}/_{16}$" x 8$^9/_{16}$" (sight)

This drawing bears compositional and stylistic similarities
to three paintings catalogued by Georges Wildenstein in his
book *The Paintings of Frogonard* published in 1960 (see; #17,
Fig. 11, #18, Plate 1, #19, Plate 2).

Provenance: Private Collection, France; Private Collection,
New York; Wildenstein and Co., New York
Literature: *The Sentinal.* Rome, New York, November 23, 1960,
ill.

Jean-Honoré Fragonard
(French; 1732-1806)

20. *Nymphs and Cupids Playing on a Bed*
pen and ink and brown wash
6$^{15}/_{16}$" x 11$^{15}/_{16}$"

An old attribution, or signature, in ink appears at the lower right: *Fragonard.* Inscribed in an 18th Century hand on the verso in ink: *M. Boullée architecte Du Roy.*

Provenance: Etienne-Louis Boullée; Alfred E. Pearson, Esq.
Literature: *Catalogue of Important Old Master Drawings.* Sotheby & Co., London, July 6, 1967, #26, ill.

Jean-Honoré Fragonard
(French; 1732-1806)

21. *Susannah and the Elders*
sepia
8$^7/_{16}$" x 14$^3/_{16}$" (sight)

PROVENANCE: Jombert père, Paris; F. Villot, Paris; Hippolyte
Walferdin, Paris; Albert Hecht, Paris; E. Pontremoli, Paris;
Wildenstein and Co., New York

LITERATURE: *Vente Jombert père*. Paris, April 15, 1776, #223;
Vente F. Villot. Paris, May 16-18, 1859, p. 19, #114; *Vente Walferdin*.
Hôtel Drouot, Paris, April 12-16, 1880, p. 63, #208; Portalis,
R. *Honoré Fragonard*. Paris, 1889, p. 313; Algoud, H. *Fragonard*.
Monaco, 1941, frontispiece of preface; Ananoff, Alexandre.
L'Oeuvre dessiné de Jean-Honoré Fragonard. Paris, Vol. I, 1961,
p. 70, #100, fig. 45, Vol. II, 1963, p. 298, #100.

EXHIBITED: Jacques Seligmann & Fils, Paris. *Exposition de
dessins de Fragonard*. May 9-30, 1931, cat. #46; Wildenstein & Co.,
London. *Drawings by the Masters, XVth to XIXth Centuries*.
October 5-30, 1960, p. 7, cat. #28.

HENRY FUSELI
(Swiss; 1741-1825)

22. *The Conversion of Saint Paul*
1778, dated
brown ink and wash
7″ x 11½″ (sight)

Signed and dated at the lower right: *? Fusely Rome 1778.*

Dr. Gert Schiff states that this drawing, depicting the future
saint lying on a tombstone dedicated by the Christians to a
martyr called Damasippos, is part of Fuseli's "Roman Album".
There is an almost identical version of this composition dated
1770 in the British Museum.

PROVENANCE: Dr. Peter Nathan, Zurich; St. Julian Fishburne,
New Paltz; Richard Feigen Gallery, New York
LITERATURE: The drawing will be included in Dr. Schiff's
supplement to his catalogue raisonné of Henry Fuseli's work.

ΣΑΜΑΞΙΤΗΝ ΜΑΡΤΥΡΙ
ΙΟ: ΧΡΙΣΤΟΣ

Fuzely   Rome 1775

HENRY FUSELI
(Swiss; 1741-1825)

23. *Midnight*
(1765)
pen and ink and sepia wash
8¼″ x 13″

Dr. Gert Schiff agrees with the attribution of this drawing to
Fuseli and suggests that it was done around 1764 when Fuseli
was in Barth, Swedish Pommerania with Spalding, the
Protestant theologian.

PROVENANCE: Anthony D'Offay Fine Art, London
LITERATURE: The drawing will be included in Dr. Schiff's
supplement to his catalogue raisonné of Henry Fuseli's work.

Thomas Gainsborough
(British; 1727-1788)

24. *A Herdsman Driving Cattle*
black chalk and grey wash with white chalk
9½" x 12⅝" (sight)

Literature: *Catalogue of Fine English Eighteenth and Nineteenth Century Drawings and Paintings.* Sotheby & Co., London, November 24, 1965, #27.

JEAN-BAPTISTE GREUZE
(French; 1725-1805)

25. *The Father's Curse — The Ungrateful Son*
grey wash
18⅞" x 24⁷/₁₆" (sight)

Signed at the lower right in ink: *J. B. Greuze.*

This drawing is a finished study or a copy of the composition of
Greuze's painting in the Louvre, #371. Greuze did a number of
studies for and variations on this theme which are now in the
collections of the Albertina, the Louvre, the Metropolitan
Museum, New York, and various private collections.

PROVENANCE: Vente Thibaudeau, 1857 (?); Baronne Salomon de
Rothschild; Rene Fribourg; Harry Spiro; ACA Heritage
Gallery, New York
LITERATURE: *Catalogue of French Drawings of the 18th and 19th
Centuries.* Sotheby & Co., London, October 16, 1963, #548, ill.
EXHIBITED: Palais de Charlottenborg, Copenhagen. *Exposition
de l'art Français au XVIIIe Siècle.* 1935, cat. #391.

JEAN-BAPTISTE GREUZE
(French; 1725-1805)

26. *The Happy Family*
(1766)
black chalk and grey wash
12" x 9¾"

This drawing is one of several which Greuze did of this subject. Others are in Hamburg, Narbonne, Besançon, at the Albertina in Vienna, and at the Académie de Beaux-Arts de Saint Petersbourg. In his catalogue raisonné of Greuze paintings and drawings, J. Martin states that Greuze executed the Hamburg drawing in 1766 for Wille who then gave it to Jean-Michel Moreau to engrave. Although this drawing and the one in Besançon are in the same sense as the engraving, the Hamburg drawing is most similar to the engraving in details.

LITERATURE: Smith, John. *A Catalogue Raisonné of the Works of the Most Eminent Dutch, Flemish, and French Painters.* London, 1837, Vol. 8, p. 439, #151; *Catalogue of Fine Old Master Drawings.* Sotheby & Co., London, July 7, 1966, #102.

FRANCESCO GUARDI
(Italian; 1712-1793)

27. *Christ and the Centurion*
(1758)
pen and brown ink over red chalk
19¾" x 15¼"

James Byam Shaw, who has said that this drawing is one of the
largest and most important of Guardi's adaptations, dates it
circa 1758. It is based on the Veronese painting of the same
subject of which there are three known versions, in Kansas
City, in the Prado, and at Dresden. Guardi's immediate model
seems to have been a small engraving published by Ph. Andr.
Killian in 1758. It is possible, however, that Guardi saw the
Dresden version of Veronese's painting as it was in the Casa
Grimandi de'Servi in Venice until 1748.

PROVENANCE: Private 18th century Venetian and Milanese
Collections; Seiferheld and Co., New York
LITERATURE: *Weinmüller Sale Catalogue*. Munich, October 14,
1938, Lot 344, ill.; Leporini, Heinrich. "Die Versteigerung von
Handzeichnungen bei A. Weinmüller, Munich." *Pantheon.*
October, 1938, p. 330.

Veduta della Chiesa Ducale e della Piazza di San Marco.

FRANCESCO GUARDI
(Italian; 1712-1793)

28. *View of the Chiesa Ducale and the Piazza di San Marco*
(1780)
pen and brown ink and grey wash
24$^{7}/_{16}$" x 14$^{5}/_{8}$"

Signed in ink at the lower left: *Franco Guardi delin.: e pin:*.
Inscribed in ink at the center of the bottom edge: *Veduta della Chiesa Ducale e della Piazza di San Marco.*

Professors Antonio Morassi and Rodolfo Pallucchini agreed that this drawing was executed for the purpose of being engraved as evidenced by the legend at the lower left and the space at the right left free for the engraver's name. Professor Morassi, who commented on the fresh and spirited treatment of the figures and the architecture, assigned the work to Guardi's maturity, around 1780.

PROVENANCE: M. Knoedler & Co., New York

GIACOMO GUARDI
(Italian; 1764-1835)

29. *A Venetian Courtyard*
pen and brown and black ink with grey wash
17⅞" x 11⅞" (sight)

LITERATURE: *Catalogue of Important Old Master Drawings.*
Sotheby & Co., London, November 11, 1965, #100, ill.
EXHIBITED: Alfred Brod Gallery, London. *Exhibition of Old
Master Drawings.* January 31-February 21, 1963, cat. #36, ill. p. 20.

GIACOMO GUARDI
(Italian; 1764-1835)

30. *A View of the River Brenta, with the Burchiello*
pen and ink and grey wash
4⅝″ x 8⅛″ (sight)

PROVENANCE: Margot Carnegie-Pierce, London
LITERATURE: *Catalogue of Important Old Master Drawings.*
Sotheby & Co., London, November 11, 1965, #101.

IL GUERCINO (GIOVANNI FRANCESCO BARBIERI)
(Italian; 1591-1666)

31. *Landscape with Five Figures*
pen and brown ink
7⅜″ x 10½″

Inscribed at the lower left in ink: *Guercin.* Stamp of the H. E. Field Collection at the lower right (Lugt supplement 1287).

Before this drawing was exhibited at the John Herron Art Museum in 1955 (see below) Denis Mahon stated that he accepted its attribution to Il Guercino.

PROVENANCE: H. E. Field, New York; Prouté, Paris; Mr. and Mrs. Robert Laurent, Indiana; ACA Heritage Gallery, New York
EXHIBITED: John Herron Art Museum, Indianapolis. *European Old Master Drawings in Indiana Collections.* March 6-April 10, 1955, cat. #24, ill.

Il Guercino (Giovanni Francesco Barbieri)
(Italian; 1591-1666)

32. *Study of a Seated Prophet*
red crayon and red-brown wash
10³/₁₆″ x 7⁷/₁₆″ (sight)

An ink inscription, *Guercino da Cento,* at the center of the
bottom edge is covered by the mat. The drawing is made up of
two pieces of paper.

Provenance: This drawing was previously in the collection of
Mrs. J. E. Colborne-Mackrell who inherited it from her father
who lived in Hampstead, England. It is not known how he
acquired it.
Literature: *Catalogue of Important Old Master Drawings.*
Sotheby & Co., London, November 11, 1965, #50, ill.

STUDIO OF IL GUERCINO
(Giovanni Francesco Barbieri)
(Italian; 17th Century)

33. *Diana*
pen and sepia ink
6^{15}/$_{16}$″ x 9⅜″ (sight)

PROVENANCE: This drawing, once in the collection of the
Viennese sculptor and engraver Joseph Daniel Böhm (1794-
1865), was acquired by the Avnets in 1967 from the Swetzoff
Gallery in Boston.

JAN JOSEF HOREMANS, THE ELDER
(Flemish; 1682-1759)

34. *Studies of a Young Horseman*
black chalk on grey paper
10⅜" x 7$\frac{1}{16}$"

PROVENANCE: Swetzoff Gallery, Boston

Jean-Baptiste Marie Huet
(French; 1745-1811)

35. *Shepherds*
1782, dated
pen and watercolour
7¾" x 5½" (sight)

Signed and dated at the middle right in ink: *J. B. Huet 1782.*

Provenance: Dr. Rothmann; Wildenstein and Co., London

JEAN AUGUSTE DOMINIQUE INGRES
(French; 1780-1867)

36. *Louis-Pierre Haudebourt*
(1817)
pencil
9¹/₁₆″ x 6⅝″

Signed in pencil at the lower right: *Ingres*. Inscribed in pencil
at the lower right: *a son ami Hautbourt*.

Ingres executed this portrait of his architect friend while in
Rome around 1817. It was engraved by Charreyre in 1896.

PROVENANCE: Louis-Pierre Haudebourt; Breithmeyer; Georges
Duplessis, Paris; Mme. Veuve G. Duplessis, Paris; Mathey,
Paris; Galerie Charpentier; Sacha Guitry; J. Bernadough,
Esq., London; A. Stein; Walter Fieilchenfeld, Zurich; Private
Collection, Paris; Bianchini Gallery, New York
LITERATURE: *Vente Breithmeyer*. Paris, March 1, 1869, #57;
Duplessis, Georges. *Les Portraits dessinés par Jean Auguste
Dominique Ingres*. Paris, 1896, #11, ill.; Lapauze, Henry. *Les
Dessins de Jean Auguste Dominique Ingres du Musée de Montauban*.
Paris, 1901, p. 266, mentioned after the engraving; *Vente Mme.
Veuve G. Duplessis*. Paris, March 16, 1917, #36; Galerie
Charpentier, Anonymous Sale, June 9-10, 1953, #105; *Catalogue
of Fine Old Master Drawings*. Sotheby & Co., London, July 7,
1966, #107a; "International Art Market Trends in New York,
London, and Paris." *Realités*. February, 1968, p. 13, ill.

Jean Auguste Dominique Ingres
(French; 1780-1867)

37. *Mlle. Louise Dubreuil*
1834, dated
pencil
$7^3/_{16}$" x $5^7/_{16}$"

Signed and inscribed at the lower left in pencil: *Ingres del.*
notre chère niece Louise Dubreuil. Inscribed at the lower right in
pencil: *Paris 1834.*

The sitter was the niece of the artist's wife.

PROVENANCE: Henry Lapauze, Paris; Marlborough-Gerson
Gallery, New York
LITERATURE: Lapauze, Henry. *Ingres, sa Vie et son Oeuvre.*
Paris, 1911, p. 319, ill.
EXHIBITED: Paris. *Ingres Exhibition.* 1911; Staatens Museum fra
Kunst, Stockholm. *Franske Haanstegninger fra det 19 og 20
Jarhundert.* May, 1939, cat. #72, Plate 11; Marlborough Fine Art
Ltd., London. *19th and 20th Century Watercolours, Drawings,
and Sculpture.* January-February, 1963, cat. #32; Nat. Kunst-
museum, Stockholm. "Ingres." 1965; Marlborough-Gerson
Gallery, New York. *French drawings.* January, 1966, cat. #57, ill.

JEAN AUGUSTE DOMINIQUE INGRES
(French; 1780-1867)

38. *Portrait of the Banker Laffitte*
1819, dated
pencil
9$^5/_{16}$" x 7$^7/_{16}$" (sight)

Signed and dated at the lower left in pencil: *Ingres 1819.*

This is a study for a portrait which Ingres was commissioned
to execute for Laffitte, an important figure in Parisian society
and banking during the early 19th Century. It is said that
Laffitte was unsatisfied with the drawing and therefore refused
to honor the commission for the oil. It was not until after the
death of both men that the heirs of Laffitte, realising the merit
of the artist, paid for the drawing.

PROVENANCE: David Bassine, New York

JEAN-BAPTISTE ISABEY
(French; 1767-1855)

39. *Gentleman Smoking a Pipe*
black pencil heightened with white
10¼″ x 7¾″ (sight)

PROVENANCE: Wildenstein and Co., London

JEAN-BAPTISTE ISABEY
(French; 1767-1855)

40. *Lady Seated at a Window*
black pencil heightened with white
$10^{5}/_{16}$″ x $7^{7}/_{8}$″ (sight)

PROVENANCE: Wildenstein and Co., London

Attributed to
HANS SEBALD LAUTENSACK
(German; 1524-ca. 1560)

41. *River Landscape*
(1544)
pen and black and white ink on red-brown paper
8¼" x 12½"

Dated and initialled in white ink over black ink at the top
center: *1514 A D.*

There are three other drawings which various authorities have
agreed were executed by the same hand as this, two landscapes
in Darmstadt (see: *Stift und Feder.* 1928, Plates 73 & 74) and one
in Berlin (see below: Schmidt, #102). These are dated 1540.
The Avnet drawing originally had a date 1544 which was altered
at the same time the false monogram of Dürer was added.

PROVANENCE: V. E. Rodregues, Paris; Henry Oppenheimer,
Esq., England; Bonde, Vienna; R. M. Light and Co., Boston
LITERATURE: *Catalogue d'un Vente Importante de Dessins Anciens,
Collection R...(V. E. Rodrigues), de Paris....* Frederick Muller &
Cie., July 12-13, 1921, #80, Plate LXXXI; *Catalogue of the Famous
Collection of Old Master Drawings Formed by the Late Henry
Oppenheimer, Esq., F. S. A.* Christie, Manson and Woods, Ltd.,
London, July 10, 13, 14, 1936, #391; van de Wall, H. "Graphische
Arbeiten des Monogrammisten P. S." *Graphische Künst.* 1939,
N. F. IV, p. 47ff; Schmidt, Annegrit. "Hans Lautensack."
Nürnberger Forschungen, Vol. IV, Nürnberg, 1957, #110.

Sir Thomas Lawrence
(British; 1769-1830)

42. *Lady with a Lute*
pen and ink
7½" x 5½" (sight)

Inscribed along the bottom edge: *Drawn by Sir T. Lawrence P. R. A.*

Provenance: George Gray; Melville Gray, Perth
Literature: *Catalogue of Eighteenth and Nineteenth Century Paintings and Drawings.* Sotheby & Co., London, October 27, 1965, #106.

Drawn by Sir T Lawrence P R A

PIETRO LONGHI
(Italian; 1702-1785)

43. *A Venetian Coffee House*
brown ink and wash
7¾" x 11¼"

PROVENANCE: John Skippe, England; Mrs. A. C. Raynor Wood,
England; Edward Holland Martin; The Art Institute of Chicago
(Gift of the Joseph and Helen Regenstein Foundation);
Wildenstein and Co., New York
LITERATURE: The Vasari Society for the Reproduction of Draw-
ings by Old Masters. 1906-1907, Part II, Plate 13; Frohlich-Bume,
L. "Alte Handzeichnungen en Bei Christie's London." *Welt-
kunst.* Vol. XXVIII, No. 22, November 15, 1958, p. 13; *Catalogue
of the Well-Known Collection of Old Master Drawings Formed in
the 18th Century by John Skippe now in the Property of Edward
Holland Martin, Esq.* Christie, Manson and Woods Ltd., London,
November 20-21, 1958, ill.; *The Annual Report.* The Art Institute
of Chicago, 1960-1961, p. 11.
EXHIBITED: Birmingham Museum and Art Gallery, Birmingham,
England. *Commemorative Exhibition of the Treasures of the
Midlands.* 1934, p. 57, cat. #215; Burlington Fine Arts Club,
Burlington, England, 1938; Royal Academy of Arts, London.
Drawings by Old Masters. August 13-October 25, 1953, p. 50,
cat. #193.

PIETRO LONGHI
(Italian; 1702-1785)

44. *A Venetian Wineshop*
brown ink and wash
8″ x 11⅛″

PROVENANCE: John Skippe, England; Mrs. A. C. Raynor Wood,
England; Edward Holland Martin; The Art Institute of Chicago
(Gift of the Joseph and Helen Regenstein Foundation);
Wildenstein and Co., New York
LITERATURE: *Catalogue of the Well-Known Collection of Old
Master Drawings formed in the 18th Century by John Skippe now
in the Property of Edward Holland Martin, Esq.* Christie, Manson
and Woods Ltd., London, November 20-21, 1959, ill.; *The Annual
Report.* The Art Institute of Chicago, 1960-1961, p. 11.
EXHIBITED: Birmingham Museum and Art Gallery, Birmingham,
England. *Commemorative Exhibition of the Treasures of the
Midlands.* 1934, p. 56, cat. #213.

MELCHIOR LORCK
(Danish; 1526/7-ca. 1583)

45. *Eight Ladies in Ancient Costumes*
(1571-73)
pen and ink
8½" x 12³⁄₁₆"

Signed with the artist's monogram on the hood of the fourth woman from the right: *MLF.* Inscribed on the third woman from the left: *SACHSEN.* Seven of the women are marked with either an *F* or an *I,* probably referring to inscriptions now cut off.

PROVENANCE: John Evelyn, England; J. H. C. Evelyn
LITERATURE: Ward-Jackson, Peter. "Some Rare Drawings by Melchior Lorich." *The Connoisseur.* March, 1955, #46, ill.; Fischer, Erick. *Melchior Lorck.* Royal Museum of Fine Arts, Copenhagen, 1962, #78, ill.; *Catalogue of Important Old Master Drawings.* Sotheby & Co., London, March 15, 1966, #16, ill.
EXHIBITED: Royal Museum of Fine Arts, Copenhagen, 1962.

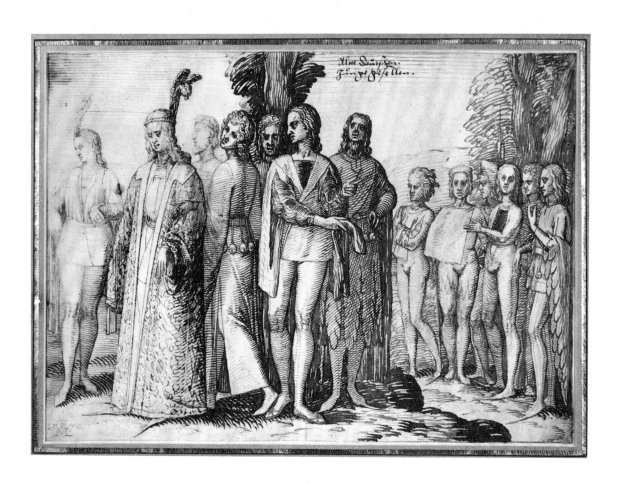

MELCHIOR LORCK
(Danish; 1526/7-ca. 1583)

46. *Young Men in Ancient German Costumes*
1570, dated
pen and brown ink and brown wash
9⅞" x 13¹⁵/₁₆" (sight)

Signed with the artist's monogram and dated at the lower left:
15 MLF 70. Inscribed near the upper edge: *Altte Deutchen.
Junge gesellen.*

PROVENANCE: John Evelyn, England; J. H. C. Evelyn; R. M.
Light and Co., Boston
LITERATURE: Ward-Jackson, Peter. "Some Rare Drawings by
Melchior Lorich." *The Connoisseur.* March, 1955, #46, ill.;
Fischer, Erick. *Melchior Lorck.* Royal Museum of Fine Arts,
Copenhagen, 1962, #68, ill.; *Catalogue of Important Old Master
Drawings.* Sotheby & Co., London, March 15, 1966, #6, ill.
EXHIBITED: Royal Museum of Fine Arts, Copenhagen, 1962.

The following twenty drawings are copies of lost drawings by
MELCHIOR LORCK.

PROVENANCE: All of these drawings after Lorck were part of the
John Evelyn Collection, England.
LITERATURE: Ward-Jackson, Peter. "Some Rare Drawings by
Melchior Lorich." *The Connoisseur.* March, 1955, #8-#12, #14,
#15, #19-#31, (#52 and #56 are illustrated); Fischer, Erick.
Melchior Lorck. Royal Museum of Fine Arts, Copenhagen,
1962, #29-#35, #37-#48, #50 (all are illustrated); *Catalogue of
Important Old Master Drawings.* Sotheby & Co., London, March
15, 1966, Lot nos. 20-30 (#47, #56, #57 and #61 are illustrated).
EXHIBITED: All of these drawings after Lorck were exhibited at
the Royal Museum of Fine Arts, Copenhagen, 1962.

AFTER MELCHIOR LORCK
47. *A Turkish Soldier Carrying a Quiver Full of Arrows and a Bow*
pen and ink and brown wash
$9^{1}/_{16}''$ x $6^{5}/_{16}''$

Inscribed at the top in black ink: *Sypaheler.*

AFTER MELCHIOR LORCK
48. *A Turkish Soldier in a Helmet, Holding a Mace and Battle Axe*
(early 17th century)
pen and ink and brown wash
$9^{11}/_{16}''$ x $6^{3}/_{8}''$

AFTER MELCHIOR LORCK
49. *Back View of a Turkish Soldier Holding a Mace*
pencil and brown wash
$7^{5}/_{8}''$ x $5^{5}/_{16}''$

AFTER MELCHIOR LORCK
50. *A Turkish Soldier in a Soft Hat, Holding a Mace and a Battle Axe*
(early 17th century)
brown wash
$9^{5}/_{16}''$ x $6^{15}/_{16}''$

47.

48.

49.

50.

Ein Rische Jungfrauen Tochterlein
von 8 Jar.

51.

Ein Rische Jun...
von 8 od...

52.

53.

AFTER MELCHIOR LORCK

51. *An Eight Year Old Turkish Girl*
pencil and brown wash
$7^{3}/_{16}''$ x $4^{7}/_{8}''$

Inscribed along the top in black ink: *Turckische Jungfrauw.*
Tochterlein. von 8 Jar.

AFTER MELCHIOR LORCK

52. *A Turkish Boy About Eight Years Old*
brown wash
$7^{3}/_{8}''$ x $5^{1}/_{8}''$

Inscribed at the upper right in black ink: *Turckische Jung . . . .*
von 8 oder . . . .

AFTER MELCHIOR LORCK

53. *A Turkish Soldier, Holding a Bow and Arrow, Seen from Behind*
brown wash
$7^{1}/_{4}''$ x $5^{9}/_{16}''$

54.

55.

56.

57.

AFTER MELCHIOR LORCK

54. *Back View of a Gesticulating Turk*
(early 17th century)
pen and ink and brown wash
9$\frac{1}{16}$" x 6$\frac{1}{4}$"

Inscribed at the upper left in black ink: *Turckischen Keysers Stockh Narr.*

AFTER MELCHIOR LORCK

55. *A Turkish Soldier Holding a Mace, a Spear and a Shield*
brown wash
9$\frac{11}{16}$" x 6$\frac{3}{8}$"

Inscribed at the upper right in black ink: *Arkanschy.*

AFTER MELCHIOR LORCK

56. *A Turkish Soldier in a Turban, Holding a Spear and a Mace*
(early 17th century)
pen and black ink and brown wash
8$\frac{15}{16}$" x 5$\frac{3}{4}$"

Inscribed at the upper left in black ink: *Turcken an den grenntzen der Persern.*

AFTER MELCHIOR LORCK

57. *A Turkish Soldier, His Hands Folded over his Stomach*
(early 17th century)
pencil and brown wash
8$\frac{5}{16}$" x 6"

AFTER MELCHIOR LORCK

58. *A Turkish Soldier with a Leopard Skin, and a Man in a Long Cloak*
pencil and brown wash
10⅛″ x 7⅛″

AFTER MELCHIOR LORCK

59. *A Lady, Seen from Behind, Carrying a Child*
pencil and brown wash
10⅛″ x 5⅞″

Inscribed at the top in black ink: *Ein Turckische Magdt tragt auff ihrer Achselen ein Kindelein.*

AFTER MELCHIOR LORCK

60. *Four Young Turkish Girls*
pencil and brown wash
7¹³/₁₆″ x 12″

Inscribed in black ink above the three girls on the left: *Turckische Döchterlein. Magdtlein. Junckfrawlein und Kinder.* Inscribed in black ink above the girl on the right: *Ein Turckische Junck fraw, ein Magdtlein.*

AFTER MELCHIOR LORCK

61. *A Turkish Soldier in a Helmet, Holding a Spear and a Shield*
(early 17th century)
pencil and brown wash
7½″ x 4⁷/₁₆″

AFTER MELCHIOR LORCK

62. *Two Young Turkish Girls*
(early 17th century)
pencil and brown wash
7½″ x 11¹/₁₆″

Inscribed in black ink above the girl on the left: *Turckische Jungkfraw.* Inscribed in black ink above the girl on the right: *ein Magdtlein oder Turckische Jungfraw.*

58.

59.

60.

61.

62.

AFTER MELCHIOR LORCK

63. *An Adscript Servant Woman*
(early 17th century)
pencil, pen and black ink and brown wash
9³/₁₆″ x 5³/₄″

Inscribed along the top in black ink in a hand different from the others: *Eine Turkische arme dirn oder Magdtt, oder eine Leibeigene, die einer Reichen frawen dienet, also sie auch bey den Moren und Arabier gekleidett in Jhrem habit gehen.*

AFTER MELCHIOR LORCK

64. *Three Adscript Servant Women*
(early 17th century)
pen and ink and brown wash
8⁷/₈″ x 5¹³/₁₆″

Inscribed along the top in black ink: *Ein armes weib und zwey andre Arme Leibeigene dienst Magdt oder Resenanicpi (?).*

AFTER MELCHIOR LORCK

65. *Three Dervishes*
(early 17th century)
pen and ink and brown wash
8¹⁵/₁₆″ x 6³/₁₆″

Inscribed along the top in black ink: *So sein die Turckische Munche.*

AFTER MELCHIOR LORCK

66. *Two Christian Prisoners*
pencil and pen and black ink
9³/₈″ x 6⁵/₁₆″

Inscribed along the top in black ink: *Arme gefangene Christen, gehen so lange Aneiñander mitt einer Ketten Zusammen geschmidett, und bettelen bis sie bezalen, was sie Schuldich seinn.*

63.

64.

65.

66.

NICOLAES MAES
(Dutch; 1632-1693)

67. *A Young Woman Attending to her Child*
pen and ink with grey and brown washes
6½" x 7¾"

Stamp of the Pierre Crozat (?) Collection at the lower right
(Lugt 474).

PROVENANCE: Pierre Crozat (?), Paris; George Biorklund
LITERATURE: *Catalogue of Important Old Master Drawings*.
Sotheby & Co., London, March 15, 1966, #78, ill.

CARLO MARATTI
(Italian; 1625-1713)

68. *Study for Saint Charles Borromeo*
red and white chalks with touches of black chalk
14¹⁵/₁₆″ x 8⁹/₁₆″

Stamp of the Jonathan Richardson Collection at the lower
right (Lugt 2184).

This drawing is a study for the figure of the Saint which appears
in the altarpiece "Madonna with Saint Ignatius and Saint
Charles Borromeo" at S. Maria in Vallicella in Rome which was
painted circa 1685 (see: Waterhouse, Ellis. *Baroque Painting in
Rome, The Seventeenth Century.* London, 1937, p. 80). Another
study for same figure, showing only the drapery, is in the Royal
Collection at Windsor Castle (see: Blunt, Sir Anthony and
Hereward Lester Cooke. *Roman drawings of the XVII & XVIII
Centuries in the Collection of H. M. the Queen at Windsor Castle.*
London, 1960, #287, Plate 58). Studies for the whole composition
of the altarpiece are in the Albertina and at Copenhagen.

PROVENANCE: Jonathan Richardson, London
LITERATURE: *Catalogue of Important Old Master Drawings.*
Sotheby & Co., March 15, 1966, #40, ill.

Jean-Michel Moreau (Moreau the Younger)
(French; 1741-1814)

69. *Invitation to a Ball*
pen and brown ink and wash
4³/₁₆″ x 5½″ (sight)

Signed at the lower left in ink: *Moreau*. Stamp of the Alfred
Beurdeley Collection at the lower left (Lugt 421). Inscribed in
ink and wash at the center: *BAL PARÉ à Versailles POUR LE
MARIAGE de Monseigneur Le Dauphin Le* _____.

Provenance: M. Maherault, Paris; G. Mülbacher, Paris; Alfred
Beurdeley, Paris; McRoberts and Tunnard Limited, London
Literature: *Vente Maherault*. Paris, May 27-29, 1880, #186, ill.;
Vente Mülbacher. Galerie Georges Petit, Paris, May 15-18, 1899,
#207; *Vente Beurdeley*. Galerie Georges Petit, Paris, March 13-15,
1905, #172.
Exhibited: Exposition Universelle — Retrospective de la Ville
de Paris. Paris, 1900, #202.

LOUIS-GABRIEL MOREAU (MOREAU THE ELDER)
(French; 1740-1806)

70. *Figures in a Park*
watercolour
7³/₈" x 11"

PROVENANCE: Mrs. Joseph Regenstein; The Art Institute of
Chicago; Wildenstein and Co., New York
LITERATURE: *The Annual Report.* The Art Institute of Chicago.
1960-1961, p. 11.

GIOVANNI LORENZO BERNINI
(Italian; 1598-1680)

cover, 4.
Portrait of a Young Man (Self-Portrait)
black and red chalk, heightened with white chalk
12⁷/₁₆" x 9"

Inscribed in pencil at lower right: *da Cav. Bernini.*

Frederico Zeri suggests that this is a self-portrait and dates
it circa 1618 by comparing it to portraits at Windsor and the
British Museum (see: Brauer, H. and R. Wittkower. *Die Zeich-
nungen des Gianlorenzo Bernini.* Berlin, 1931, Plates 1 & 2). The
catalogue of the Morgan Library exhibition (see below) suggests
that "attention should also be drawn to the more striking
resemblance to the portrait in the Brera at Milan, which
Wittkower has put forth as the earliest self-likeness of the artist,
dating it about 1610-1612 (*Burlington Magazine,* XCIII, 1951, p. 55,
fig. 16)....Assuming the boy in the Brera portrait to be between
twelve and fourteen years old, and the Avnet youth several
years further into his teens, one would arrive at a date of
about 1614 or 1615 for the present drawing."

PROVENANCE: Wildenstein and Co., New York
LITERATURE: *Art News.* Vol. 57, No. 54, Summer, 1958, p. 17, ill.;
Zeri, Frederico. "Gian Lorenzo Bernini: Un Marmo dimenticato
e un disegno." *Paragone,* Vol. IX, No. 115, 1959, pp. 63-4, Plate 42.
EXHIBITED: Wildenstein and Co., New York. *A Comprehensive
Exhibition of Drawings and Watercolors.* Summer, 1958, cat. #14;
Pierpont Morgan Library, New York. *Drawings from New York
Collections, II, The Seventeenth Century in Italy.* February 23-
April 22, 1967, cat. #67, ill.

GEORGE MORLAND
(British; 1763-1804)

71. *Portrait of John Graham*
pencil and chalk
$10^{15}/_{16}$" x $7^{15}/_{16}$" (sight)

Signed at the right edge in pencil: *G. Morland.*

PROVENANCE: Swetzoff Gallery, Boston

JEAN-MARC NATTIER, THE YOUNGER
(French; 1685-1766)

72. *Venus and Adonis*
(1713)
wash
11³/₄" x 9⁷/₈"

This drawing is a study for a painting of the same subject
signed and dated 1713. The painting was formerly in the
collection of the Comte de Gramont and is reproduced in the
catalogue of the sale of that collection at Galerie Charpentier on
June 15, 1934 (No. 34).

PROVENANCE: Jules Féral; Wildenstein and Co., London
EXHIBITED: Wildenstein and Co., London. *The Art of Drawing*.
May 9-June 16, 1956, p. 19, cat. #65.

ADRIAEN OR ISAAC VAN OSTADE
(Dutch; 1610-1684; 1621-1649)

73. *Dancing Peasant*
pen and brown ink and wash
(oval) 8″ x 5¼″

Attribution on the mount: *Ad. van Ostade.*

Prior to its exhibition at the John Herron Art Museum in 1955
(see below) Léo van Puyvelde stated that he agreed with the
old attribution to Adriaen whereas De Vries suggested Isaac.

PROVENANCE: T. Lawrence; Prouté, Paris; Mr. and Mrs. Robert
Laurent, Indiana; ACA Heritage Gallery, New York
EXHIBITED: John Herron Art Museum, Indianapolis. *European
Old Master Drawings in Indiana Collections.* March 6-April 10,
1955, cat. #33, ill.

Jacopo Palma, the Younger
(Italian; 1544-1628)

74. *Christ Led to the Cross*
pen and brown ink
$7^{7}/_{8}"$ x 7"

PROVENANCE: J. Peoli, London; Seiferheld and Co., New York;
Bianchini Gallery, New York

Bartolomeo Passarotti
(Italian; 1529-1592)

75. *Study of a Hand*
pen and sepia ink
7" x 9½"

Provenance: Dr. Carl Robert Rudolf, London;
Swetzoff Gallery, Boston

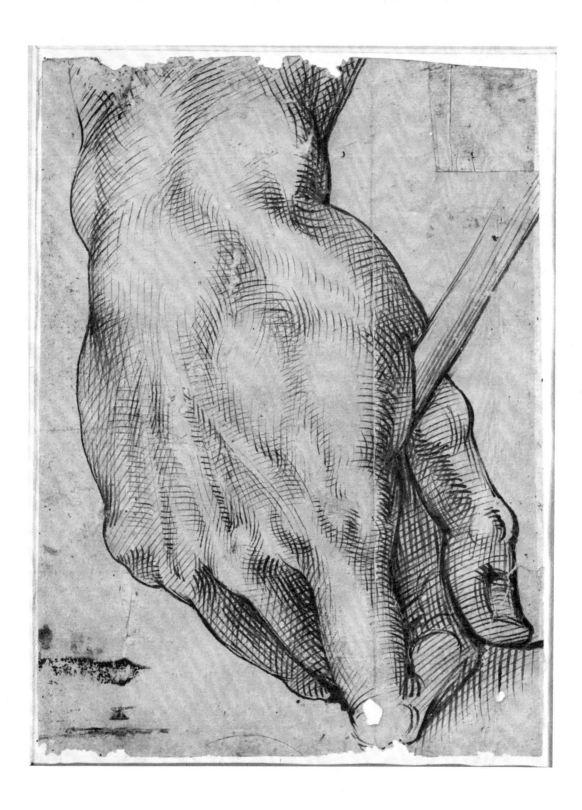

GUISEPPE PIATTOLI
(Italian; 18th century)

76. *Ladies and Gentlemen Seated in a Drawing Room Playing a Game*
pen and ink and brown wash
8¾" x 12⅜"

LITERATURE: *Catalogue of Important Old Master Drawings.*
Sotheby & Co., London, March 15, 1966, #47, ill.

Pieter Jansz Quast
(Dutch; 1606-1647)

78. *The Rich Man Beset by Fools*
1640/1641, dated
pencil on vellum
10⅜" x 15¹¹/₁₆" (sight)

Signed and dated at the upper right in pencil: *Pieter Quast.f.1640.*
Signed and dated at the lower right in ink: *Peter Quast.f.1641.*
Stamp of the H. C. Valkema Blouw Collection at the lower left
(Lugt 2505).

Jean Baptiste Siméon Chardin
(French; 1699-1779)

11. *Portrait of a Young Boy*
1777, dated
pastel
17³/₄" x 14³/₄" (sight)

Signed and dated at the lower right: *chardin 1777.*

12. *Portrait of a Young Girl*
1777, dated
pastel
17³/₄" x 14³/₄" (sight)

Signed and dated at the lower left: *chardin 1777.*

When these pictures were first catalogued by Guiffrey the date was incorrectly read as 1776, and this error was repeated by most of the later authors. The portraits, in fact, bear the date of 1777 and were in the Salon of that year when the artist exhibited three pictures listed as "Trois têtes d'étude au pastel sous le même numéro", (#50). The Saint-Aubin drawings of the Salon of 1777 show a head of an old man and portraits of a boy and girl, which until now had not been identified. In these tiny marginal sketches Saint-Aubin has drawn the pictures side by side like pendants. The poses clearly correspond to the Avnet pastels and one can even make out the hat worn by the boy and an indication of the chair. (See: Dacier, E. *Catalogue de ventes et livrets de salons illustrés par Gabriel de Saint-Aubin.* IV, "Livret du Salon de 1777", Paris, 1910.)

PROVENANCE: Princesse Mathilde; M. Foulon de Vaulx, Paris; Wildenstein and Co., New York
LITERATURE: Dayot, A. and L. Vaillat. *L'Oeuvre de J.-B. S. Chardin et de J.-H. Fragonard.* Paris, no date (1907), numbers 2 and 3, ill.; Guiffrey, J. "L'exposition Chardin — Fragonard", *Revue de*

l'art ancien et moderne. Vol. XXII, 1907, p. 102; Guiffrey, J. *Catalogue de l'oeuvre de J. B. Siméon Chardin*. Paris, 1908, p. 77, numbers 125 and 126; Furst, H. E. A. *Chardin*. London, 1911, p. 136; Wildenstein, Georges. *Chardin*. Paris, 1933, p. 204, #656, ill., p. 205, #667, ill.; Wildenstein, Georges. *Chardin*. Zurich, 1963, p. 219, #376, pp. 219-220, #377, ill., p. 221, #390.

EXHIBITED: Salon de 1777, Paris, #50 (See: *Collection des livrets des anciennes expositions*, Paris, 1870, p. 17); Galerie Georges Petit, Paris. *Exposition Chardin-Fragonard*. June 15-July 15, 1907, numbers 75 and 76 (catalogue reprinted in J. Guiffrey, *op. cit.*, 1908, pp. 53-54).

JEAN PILLEMENT
(French; 1728-1808)

77. RECTO: *Cartouche with Feathers, Butterflies,*
Apples and a Ribbon
gouache
13⁷/₈" x 10¹/₁₆" (sight)

PROVENANCE: McRoberts and Tunnard Limited, London

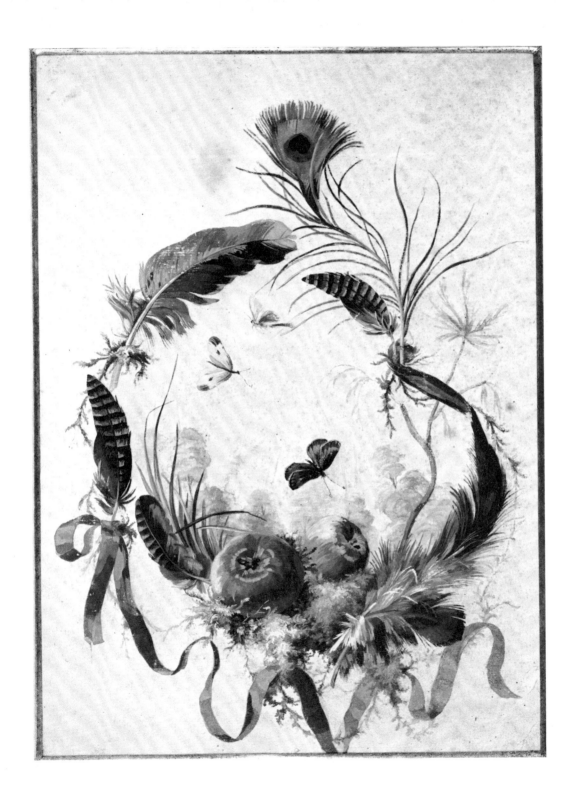

JEAN PILLEMENT
(French; 1728-1808)

77. VERSO: *Study for Chinoiserie Decoration*
gouache
13³/₁₆″ x 9³/₈″ (sight)

PROVENANCE: McRoberts and Tunnard Limited, London

PROVENANCE: H. C. Valkema Blouw, Holland; Seiferheld and Co., New York; Bianchini Gallery, New York

HUBERT ROBERT
(French; 1733-1808)

80. *Pyramid*
(1773)
sanguine with pen and wash and touches of gouache
14⁵/₁₆″ x 11³/₈″

Signed in pen on the lintel of the door of the pyramid: *H.Robert*.
Stamp of the Marius Paulme Collection at the lower right
(Lugt 1910).

A pendant to this drawing entitled "The Ancient Temple" is illustrated in the Paulme Collection auction catalogue of 1929 (see below). It is signed and bears the date 1773 which gives an approximate date for "Pyramid".

PROVENANCE: Marius Paulme, Paris; R. M. Light and Co., Boston
LITERATURE: *Catalogue des Dessins Anciens...Composant la Collection de M. Marius Paulme*. Galerie Georges Petit, Paris, May 14, 1929, p. 76, #215, Plate 145.
EXHIBITED: Galerie J. Charpentier, France. *Exposition Hubert Robert et Louis Moreau*. June, 1922, cat. #76.

Hubert Robert
(French; 1733-1808)

81. *A View of a Roman Palace*
pen and ink with blue and brown washes
tondo: 7⅝" diam.

With an old attribution, or signature, in ink at the lower left
edge: *Robert.*

Provenance: Lady Mendl; Frank Wessberg, Esq.
Literature: *Catalogue of Fine Old Master Drawings.* Sotheby &
Co., London, December 1, 1966, #70.

GEORGE ROMNEY
(British; 1734-1802)

82. *Study for the Infant Shakespeare Attended by Nature and the Passions*
(1791)
pencil
8" x 5"

Stamp of the Alfred A. de Pass Collection at the lower right (Lugt supplement 108a).

In 1791 Romney completed the oil painting "The Infant Shakespeare Attended by Nature and the Passions" and gave it to John Boydell who exhibited it in his Shakespeare Gallery. The Avnet drawing is a sketch for the composition of the oil and a study for the head of the Passion 'Hatred'.

PROVENANCE: Alfred A. de Pass, London; George Ranncey; Charles Carr, New York

GEORGE ROMNEY
(British; 1734-1802)

83. *Study of a Woman*
pen and brown ink with grey wash
14½" x 8⁹⁄₁₆"

Stamp of the Alfred A. de Pass Collection at the lower right
(Lugt supplement 108a). With a sticker: *from the A. de Pass
Collection and later in the Royal Institution of Cornwall in Truro.*
Inscribed at the upper left in pencil: *42.*

PROVENANCE: Alfred A. de Pass, London; The Royal Institution
of Cornwall, England; Swetzoff Gallery, Boston

GEORGE ROMNEY
(British; 1734-1802)

84. *Two Women, Seated and Kneeling*
pencil, pen and ink and sepia wash
11⅛″ x 9″ (sight)

PROVENANCE: Air Commodore D. W. Clapen
LITERATURE: *Catalogue of Fine English and Nineteenth Century Drawings.* Sotheby & Co., London, November 23, 1966, #273.

SALVATOR ROSA
(Italian; 1615-1673)

85. *Rinaldo and Ferraú Fighting a Duel, as Angelica Flees*
pen and bistre wash
9³/₈″ x 7¹/₁₆″

Stamp of the Charles Gasc Collection at the lower right
(Lugt 543).

This is an illustration of a scene from Ludovico Ariosto's
Orlando Furioso.

PROVENANCE: Robert Fullerton Undy, England; Charles Gasc,
Paris; McRoberts and Tunnard Limited, London

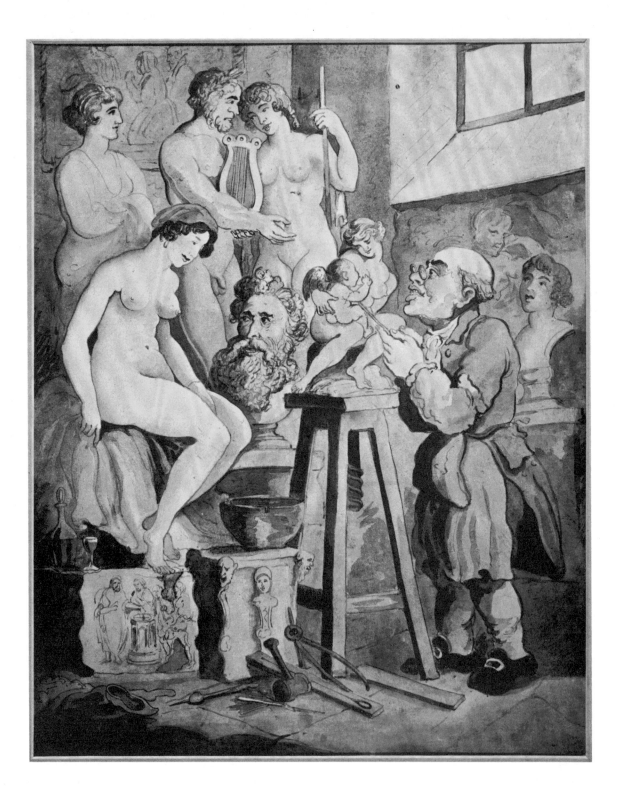

Thomas Rowlandson
(British; 1756-1827)

86. *Nollekens and his Venus*
(1800)
watercolour
14⅜″ x 11⁷⁄₁₆″ (sight)

Signed at the lower left in wash: *Rowlandson.*

Provenance: Milton Hebald, Italy
Literature: Grego, Joseph. *Rowlandson the Caricaturist.*
New York, 1880, Vol. II, pp. 16-19.

Jacob Isaakszoon van Ruisdael
(Dutch; 1628/9-1682)

87. *The Ruins of Brederode Castle*
charcoal with grey and brown washes
7½" x 10" (sight)

PROVENANCE: R. von Kühlmann
LITERATURE: *Anonymous Collection Sale*. Hollstein and Puppel,
Berlin, February 27, 1933, Lot 650, ill.; *R. von Kühlmann Collection
Sale*. Karl and Faber, Munich, April 27-29, 1959, Lot 32; *Catalogue
of Important Old Master Drawings*. Sotheby & Co., London,
March 15, 1966, #84.

Augustine de Saint-Aubin
(French; 1736-1807)

88. *Self-Portrait in Profile*
(1780)
black and white ink, charcoal, grey wash, watercolour and
gold leaf
7$\frac{1}{16}$" x 5$\frac{7}{16}$" (sight)

Inscribed at the lower center in ink: *Augustin de St. Aubin.*
Deffinateur du Roy.

Provenance: Jacques Doucet, Paris; J. G. Cogswell, New York;
Mortimer L. Schiff, New York; Alfred A. Pearson, Torquay;
Faeber and Maison, Ltd., London
Literature: Société de Reproductions des Dessins de Maîtres.
Paris, 1911, reproduced in facsimile, Plate 32; *Collection Jacques*
Doucet, Catalogue des Dessins & Pastels. Georges Petit, Paris,
1912, Vol. I, #47, ill.; *Important Pictures and Drawings by Old*
Masters. Christie, Manson and Woods, Ltd., London, June 24,
1938, #49; *Catalogue of Important Old Master Drawings*. Sotheby
& Co., London, July 6, 1967, #29.

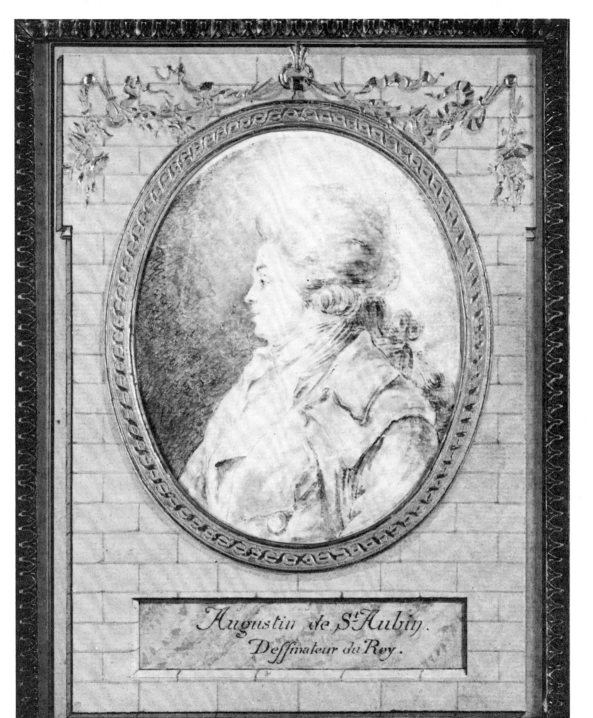

Augustin de St Aubin.
Deſſinateur du Roy.

Orazio Samacchini
(Italian; 1532-1577)

89. *The Holy Family and the Infant Saint John*
pen and ink heightened with white body colour and light
brown wash on green paper
9½″ x 7³/₁₆″ (sight)

Stamp of the Benjamin West Collection at the lower right
(Lugt 419).

Mr. Philip Pouncey has attributed this drawing to Samacchini
and has stated that it is an almost exact study for a painting in
the Borghese Gallery in Rome which is catalogued in Paola
della Pergola's *Galleria Borghese* (Rome, 1959, Vol. II, p. 101,
No. 145, ill.).

Provenance: Benjamin West, London; McRoberts and Tunnard
Limited, London

GIOVANNI BATTISTA TIEPOLO
(Italian; 1692-1770)

90. *Madonna and Child*
pen and brown ink with grey wash over charcoal
8⁹/₁₆" x 7³/₁₆" (sight)

PROVENANCE: Edward Holland-Martin, Esq.
LITERATURE: *Pictures and Drawings by Old Masters.* Christie,
Manson and Woods, Ltd., London, May 20, 1966, #105, ill.

91. *The Baptism of Christ*
pen and brown ink and wash
11³/₁₆″ x 7³/₄″ (sight)

Signed at the lower right in ink: *Dom Tiepolo f.* Inscribed at the
upper left in ink: *4S.*

A lost painting by Giovanni Battista Tiepolo is considered to be
the source of inspiration for the group of drawings of the
Baptism of Christ executed by his son Giovanni Domenico. The
Museo Stibbert in Florence possesses Domenico's painting
connected with these studies.
The Avnet drawing was once part of an album put together
between 1783 and 1793 which bore the ex-libris of
Horace Walpole.

PROVENANCE: Horace Walpole, England; Earl Beauchamp,
England; Lucien Goldschmidt, New York
LITERATURE: Shaw, James Byam. *The Drawings of Domenico
Tiepolo*. London, 1962, pp. 33-34; *Catalogue of Drawings by
Giovanni Domenico Tiepolo*. Christie, Manson and Wood, Ltd.,
London, June 15, 1965, #7, ill.

GIOVANNI DOMENICO TIEPOLO
(Italian; 1727-1804)

92. *The Baptism of Christ*
pen and brown ink and wash
$9^{15}/_{16}''$ x $7^{5}/_{8}''$

Signed at the bottom center in ink: *Dom Tiepolo f.*

PROVENANCE: Prouté, Paris; Mr. and Mrs. Robert Laurent,
Indiana; ACA Heritage Gallery, New York
EXHIBITED: John Herron Art Museum, Indiana. *European Old
Master Drawings in Indiana Collections.* March 6-April 10, 1955,
cat. #55, ill.

GIOVANNI DOMENICO TIEPOLO
(Italian; 1727-1804)

93. *The Courtyard of a Venetian Farm*
pen and brown ink and wash, over black chalk
11″ x 15⅞″ (sight)

Signed at the lower right in ink: *Dom. Tiepolo f.* With a water-
mark similar to Heawood 867.

The stables in the background are similar to those at the Villa
Tiepolo-Duodo, Zianigo.

LITERATURE: *Catalogue of Important Old Master Drawings.*
Sotheby & Co., London, November 11, 1965, #29, ill.

GIOVANNI DOMENICO TIEPOLO
(Italian; 1727-1804)

94. *Studies of Dolphins and Seahorses*
pen and ink and brown wash
7" x 11¼"

Signed at the lower left in ink: *Dom. Tiepolo f.*

LITERATURE: *Catalogue of Important Old Master Drawings.*
Sotheby & Co., London, March 15, 1966, #44, ill.

Francesco Trevisani
(Italian; 1656-1746)

95. RECTO: *Standing Male Nude*
charcoal with white chalk on grey paper
17³/₈″ x 11″ (sight)

PROVENANCE: Milton Hebald, Italy

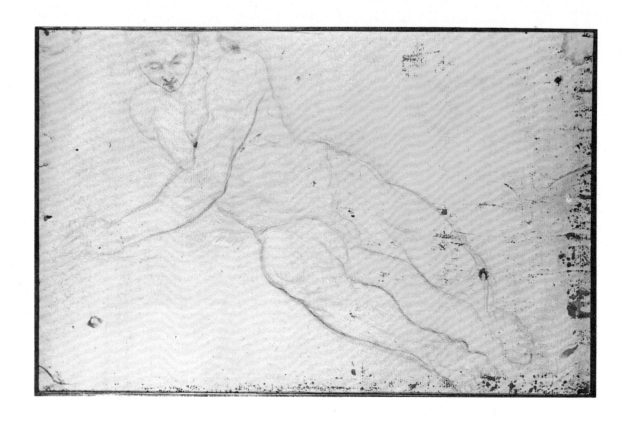

Francesco Trevisani
(Italian; 1656-1746)

95. verso: *Reclining Male Nude*
charcoal on grey paper
17³/₈ x 11″ (sight)

Provenance: Milton Hebald, Italy

Francesco Vanni
(Italian; 1563/5-1610)

96. *The Holy Family*
black chalk on light brown paper with small squaring in light
brown ink
11¼″ x 8³⁄₁₆″ (sight)

Provenance: Charles Rodgers, London; Adolph Paul Oppé,
London; McRoberts and Tunnard Limited, London

CLAUDE JOSEPH VERNET
(French; 1714-1789)

97. *An Aqueduct*
pen and ink and watercolour
12¼" x 32½" (sight)

Inscribed at the lower right in pencil: *Vernet fecit.*

PROVENANCE: Count Mycielski
LITERATURE: *Catalogue of Important Old Master Drawings.*
Sotheby & Co., London, March 15, 1966, #69.

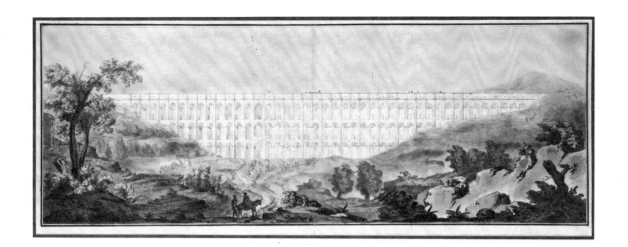

Andrea Vicentino
(Italian; ca. 1542-ca. 1617)

98. *The Ark of the Covenant Brought to the Temple*
pen and ink with brown wash heightened with white
$18^{5}/_{8}''$ x $12^{7}/_{8}''$ (sight)

PROVENANCE: John Skippe, England; John Brophy; P. & D.
Colnaghi and Co., London
LITERATURE: *The Skippe Collection of Old Master Drawings.*
Christie, Manson and Woods, Ltd., London, November 20-21,
1958, #142a (as Jacopo Palma Giovane); *Catalogue of Important
Old Master Drawings.* Sotheby & Co., London, July 8, 1964,
#112 (as Battista del Moro).

Jean Antoine Watteau
(French; 1684-1721)

99. *Two Studies of a Seated Woman*
sanguine
5⅛" x 7¾"

The figure on the right was engraved in the 18th Century by Dupuis (see: Figures of Different Characters, #210).

Provenance: Lucien Guiraud, Paris; E. V. Thaw & Co., Inc., New York

Literature: Parker, K. T. and Jacques Mathey. *Antoine Watteau; Catalogue Complet de son Oeuvre Dessiné*. Paris, 1957, #592, ill.; *Lucien Guiraud Collection Sale*. Hotel Drouot, Paris, June 14-15, 1956, #75, Plate XVII.

Exhibited: Galerie Cailleux, Paris. *Le Dessin Français de Watteau à Prud'hon*. April, 1951, cat. #162.

JEAN ANTOINE WATTEAU
(French; 1684-1721)

100. *View of Ancone*
sanguine
$6^{13}/_{16}$" x $13^{1}/_{8}$" (sight)

Inscribed at the lower left in ink: *Petite veue d'Ancone en haut de la Ville*.

PROVENANCE: Wildenstein and Co., London
LITERATURE: Parker, K. T. and J. Mathey. *Antoine Watteau; Catalogue Complet de son Oeuvre Dessiné*. Paris, 1957, #417, ill.

Petite vene d'Ancone du haut de la Ville